ITS TIME TO

Heal

You *can* develop the strength to overcome adversity and rough times.

Whatever you may have experienced in the past that has caused you emotional hurt and suffering can also be used to help you grow. Its all about the perspective by which you view it.

Healing emotionally is a process and it *is* possible. Once we overcome the stressful emotions brought on by our situations, the next step is to meet it head on. Surprisingly, our healing process can bring about a renewal in our soul and spirit.

Clear your mind from replaying the experiences over and over by facing them and replacing them. Healing is messy. Healing is hard. Healing is necessary. Healing is refreshing. The first step is to recognize the source of your pain.

Your experiences teach you about yourself. Although some experiences may be unforgettable and undeniably painful, there is an opportunity for growth. This workbook can support you in your journey of healing.

Disclaimer:
This workbook is a tool to assist you in your healing journey with reproducible worksheets. It should not be used as a substitute for a professional relationship with a mental health clinician. For more resources go to www.positivesteps10.com.

(c) 2020 All Rights Reserved.

VERSES TO

Heal

Your pain is real.

"Save me God! I am about to drown. .. But I pray to you, Lord. So when the time is right, answer me and help me with your wonderful love."
Psalms 69: 1, 13

The more you learn about yourself and make positive steps towards your healing, the more satisfied you will be with the phases in your life.

"Wisdom makes life pleasant and leads us safely along. Wisdom is a life-giving tree, the source of happiness for all who hold on to her"
Proverbs 3:17-18

We really are put in situations that we are truly strong enough to overcome. Make the choice to dig deep and learn how. You can do it! Use your adversity as an opportunity!

"We know that God is always at work for the good of everyone who loves him. They are the ones God has chosen for his purpose."
Romans 8:28

God knows your hurt. He is still with you. He knows your heart. He is waiting for you to seek Him.

"The eyes of the Lord are in every place. Watching the evil and good. "
Proverbs 15:3

REASONS TO
Heal

How do you know if this workbook is for you?

How do you know if you need to heal?

Some of the events that may cause emotional damage and pain include:
Generational scars
Loneliness
Abandonment
Rejection
Victim of trauma
Witness of trauma
Racial disparity and injustice
Emotional/verbal/mental/sexual/physical abuse
Financial turmoil
Growing up in poverty
Failed or strained relationships
Divorce
End of a long-term relationship or friendship
Death of a family member/loved one
Disappointment
And many more wounds...

This workbook is a supplemental tool to deeper work. It is not intended to stand alone.

EMOTIONS TO *Heal*

This list is in no way exhaustive, but a glimpse of why you may need healing:

Broken

Rejection

Betrayal

Inadequacy

Anger

Mental Illness

Anxiety

Digusted

Resentment

Depression

Guilt

Grief

Damaged

Hypersensitive

Addiction

Lost

Low Self-Esteem

Low Self-Confidence

Lack of feeling like you belong

Fear of failure

Overwhelmed

Emptiness

Step 1

The first step to healing is to identify what was the cause of the pain you have experienced.

The word 'Heal' is defined as "to make well again". (Merriam-Webster)

This can be from one major loss or traumatic event to a string of unpleasant events or experiences that have led you up to the point of brokenness.

You can use the next few pages to explore this step. Write or draw the source of your pain.

Consider asking yourself these questions to unpack your current situation:

- What words would I use to describe how I feel right now?
- What happened to trigger these feelings for me?
- What past hurt(s) have I experienced that has contributed to the source of these feelings?
- Is there a person, place, or thing that triggers how I feel?
- Is there a specific experience that I know is too much for me right now?
- Why am I feeling these feelings?

Heal

HEAL

HEAL

HEAL

Step 2

The next step to healing is to validate how you are feeling.

It is OK if your feelings are all over the place. Validation mainly refers to being able to accept your feelings and accepting how you perceive the situation to have impacted you. Keep how you feel in context to your experience, we often end up misplacing our emotions by taking it out on someone or something that is unrelated.

Often we try to mask our feelings or hide them because they remind us too much of the pain. However, suppressing your feelings is far worse than letting them out.

Take this moment to feel and allow yourself to express how you feel so that you can move on. Take your time. This step may need more of your attention. Write or draw it out.

Questions to consider:

- What labels would you give to your feelings right now?
- What object or colors would you use?
- How are you expressing the feelings that you have?
- Where in your body do you feel your pain?
- What coping mechanisms have you been using to deal with these feelings?
- Do you consider your coping skills as helpful or harmful?
- Identify the consequences of how you have been coping with your hurt and pain.

HEAL

HEAL

Step 3

Make a plan for how you will change some of your harmful coping habits.

For instance, if you jump from one failed relationship directly into another relationship this may have proven to be a negative choice for you. Give yourself time and space to renew yourself before committing to meeting someone else's needs. Learn more about yourself. What do you need? Are you ready to be in another relationship? What emotional scars will you be carrying into your next relationship? Who else is affected by your choice?

Write down the word HEAL with pencil or black ink in big bold letters in the middle of your next page. Then list ways you can cope better with the feelings you identified that you are experiencing in a different color over the entire page.

Questions to consider:

- Is there something that I need to do more of?
- Is there something that I need to do less of?
- Is there someone I need to take a break from or that I need to eliminate from my life?
- What is my daily routine saying about how I manage my emotions?
- Do I give myself the time to stop and think through my decisions?

HEAL

HEAL

Step 4

This step is simple. Put in the work to heal.

Use this workbook as your starter kit. Set your soul free. Forgive yourself. It is an essential part of developing self-compassion. Be willing to accept and love yourself, that is compassion.

Often unforgiveness will hinder your progress, make a point to work on this task no matter how hard it is. Forgiveness is for you, not to let the other person off of the hook. Be kind to yourself. then use the notes pages to go more in depth into how you can improve your management and decisions in those areas.

Questions to consider:

- What can I control?
- What can't I control?
- Am I focusing on things that I can control?
- What am I doing well?
- What area of weakness do I need to do more growth in?
- How will I grow in those areas?
- Am I being realistic about my goals?
- Am I willing to work towards these goals?
- Am I taking care of myself?
- Do I still need to forgive someone?
- Have I forgiven myself?
- Am I showing myself some compassion?

Positive Steps10, LLC

HEAL

HEAL

HEAL

HEAL

Step 5

Let it go.

When you hold on to past hurt, it interferes with your healing process. Get out of your own way.

Allow yourself to move on by going through the healing process. Repeat any steps that you may have felt stuck. It happens. Just like falling off of a bike, get back on and ride.

Questions to consider:
- Do I feel safe?
- Do I need to separate myself from the situation?
- Have I done steps 1-4 as outlined in this workbook?
- Am I operating in the present moment?
- Do I need a support system in this area? (consider if there is someone like a pastor, therapist, friend, or family member who can positively support you on this journey)
- How will I know when I am making progress?
- How will I deal with disappointments and setbacks in the future?
- How will you know that you have let it go?
- How will you know that you are healed?

HEAL

HEAL

HEAL

HEAL

Step 6

While we put in the work with our actions, be mindful of what you are saying to yourself. It is helpful for us to use our words to lead our thoughts and feelings. We can do this in one of two ways.

Leading yourself down a dark, scary, angry, anxious, lonely, and depressed path happens when you welcome in negative thoughts. Your thoughts will then provoke negative feelings and your actions will follow.

Isn't this why you need to heal? Instead of calling yourself demeaning names, rejecting your own accomplishments and successes, dismantling the motives behind compliments, accepting your pain and hurt as something you deserve, and adopting the "victim" and "poor me" mentality, take a time out.

Begin by leading yourself.

Tell yourself what you will do. Identify the positives you already possess. Who are you? Tell yourself, "I am..." Encourage yourself by saying what you believe you will accomplish. Affirmations are extremely powerful. Use them to your advantage. Allow yourself the opportunity to renew your soul by leading yourself with your own words.

The strength of your words can set a whole mood. It can change the course of your life just by changing your mindset. Even when adversity pops up, which it will, use your affirmations to pull yourself through them.

Affirmations can be found all over the place. The Bible is a great place to find affirming words of growth and incite. Also, search the internet for quotes that may address the specific pain you are trying to heal from. Embrace positive thoughts and words as your next positive step.

Build a mantra of daily affirmations using the worksheet provided. Add to them as you heal and grow. Develop habits around them. Print out the following sheets to keep a daily visual of what you should be saying to yourself.

SELF AFFIRMATIONS

I WILL

I HAVE

I AM

I BELIEVE

SELF AFFIRMATIONS

I WILL

I HAVE

I AM

I BELIEVE

SELF AFFIRMATIONS

I WILL

I HAVE

I AM

I BELIEVE

SELF AFFIRMATIONS

I WILL

I HAVE

I AM

I BELIEVE

Notes

3 QUESTIONS TO
Heal

Use these 3 questions when you are in a moment or a situation that has triggered you:

1. What past pain have I buried that has been triggered right now?
2. How can I be present in this very moment?
3. What is this experience needing me to do right now?

Following that same situation, when you are alone and reflecting, ask yourself these follow up questions:

1. How can I lead myself back to feeling O.K.?
2. What lesson did this experience teach me about life? About myself?
3. What does healing look like for me?
4. How will I know that I am healed?

RENEW

EMOTIONS TO
Renew

When you have begun to Renew, you may experience more of the following:

Satisfied

Cared for

Understanding

Forgiven

Safe

Heard Accomplished

Validated

Ecstatic Refreshed

Focused

Peaceful

Self-Aware

Brave

Hopeful

Joy

Winning attitude

Self-Esteem

Self-Confidence

Loved

Mindful

Belonging

Humble

Lite

Courageous

ITS TIME TO
Renew

Finally!

Healing and renewing is a process. There is no definite end. We have to go through this process in order to initiate our growth.

Use the following worksheets and notes pages to examine different areas in your life. Be kind to yourself, you are doing the best you can. As you learn more, continue to work on doing your best.

This step can bring about change, creating self-awareness. You can attract what you want out of life by writing down your goals and working towards them.

Identify your successes. Your areas of growth remain to be things that you would like to work on and that is O.K. You have to know where you've been, where you are, and where you are going to renew because you don't want to repeat any old patterns that have maintained your suffering and pain.

Be optimistic, be realistic, and be specific.

"He renews our hopes..."
Psalms 147:3

Renew

What do you usually do when you are reminded of your past hurt? Is your response rational or irrational? Do you beat yourself up over what has happened to you?

An irrational thought is the inadequate use of reason. For example, statements you may say to yourself:

>"I can't get over this" and "I deserved this pain"

When you have thoughts like this, it can bring about learned helplessness. You start behaving in a way that lives up to the thoughts and words that you say to yourself. This will hinder your healing and keep you stagnant in your current state.

Unpack your responses to triggers you experience by getting the facts. When you smell that scent, hear a particular noise, or see a reminder of an undesirable event, be intentional and let yourself know that you are O.K. Pause for that moment and get the facts. The facts will provide you with the information you need to respond accordingly. Are you really in danger? Is there an actual threat to you right now? Do you have a choice right now? Have you been able to overcome situations like this in the past? What do you need to do right now? Gathering the facts will project your rational thoughts which will increase your chances of overcoming adversity.

Rational thoughts are based on facts:

>"I will get through this" or "I am worth more than that".

HOW TO
Renew

According to Merriam-Webster, Renew means
"to make like new"

To renew is also to *replace*.

Replace your old habits- the habits that mask the pain. That habit of pretending like it hasn't occurred or that you aren't deeply hurt. These habits fester in your soul until it is triggered by a new event. We will explain five positive steps to replace negative practices.

1. As stated, replace irrational thinking with *rational thoughts*. This includes overthinking through situations. Seek only the facts in the present moment.

2. Replace negative self-talk with *positive self-talk*. Use those self-affirmations to help you with this step.

3. Replace holding grudges and resentment with *forgiveness*. Choose to forgive. Set your soul free. Forgive yourself. It is an essential part of developing self-compassion.

4. Replace chaos with *self-control*. Stop harboring all of the negative energy that is attracted to you- people, situations, bad habits. Say "no" to drama. Protect your energy by *creating boundaries* for yourself.

5. Replace passivity with *assertiveness*. Communicate what you want or need when something does not align with who you are or who you want to be. You can only control this action. Stop running from fear.

Positive Steps10, LLC

This is a fresh start. You hold the power to make the changes in your life that are needed. If you are genuinely going through this workbook then you are beginning a significantly amazing process. The results will catapult a fresh and new mindset for you.

Practical activities to Renew Yourself are below:
(Also see Appendix A)

- Create a healing music playlist
- Listen to uplifting podcasts
- Create a watchlist of healing videos or movies
- Purge old memories or items
- Read books that bring about healing
- Search for Affirmations that uplift and energize
- Read bible verses that strengthen and guide
- Reach out to people who you refer to as your support system

Questions to consider:

- What will be on your healing playlist?
- What do you watch that is comforting for you?
- Do you need to put more thought and time into your self-care?
- Is your outward appearance reflecting how you feel on the inside?
- Are you holding on to old items for memories sake?
- Who do you trust?
- What is becoming clearer for you?
- What lessons have you learned from these experiences?

Notes

Evaluate

5 DIFFERENT AREAS OF YOUR LIFE

Relationship

Friendship

Financial

Career

Self-Care

The following pages will support you in this place in your journey. Be honest with yourself as you discover and dig deeper.

RELATIONSHIP GOALS

**I WILL EXPOSE MYSELF TO HEALTHY RELATIONSHIPS.
I DESERVE TO BE TREATED WITH LOVE AND RESPECT.**

Current Relationship Status:

Am I Being Treated The Way I Want To Be Treated?

Do I have the love I need? Why or Why not?

Relationship Goals:
-
-
-
-
-

Notes

RELATIONSHIP GOALS

DIG DEEPER

What do I need to feel healed in this area of my life?

How will I know that I am healed?

A few lessons Love taught me:
-
-
-
-

I forgive...

Notes

Notes

Notes

FRIENDSHIP GOALS

I WILL SURROUND MYSELF WITH POSITIVE ENERGY

Current Support System:

_____

_____

_____

What I Value In My Friend:

_____

_____

_____

Am I In The Company of Positive Energy?　　　　Yes or No

Are My Friends Trustworthy?　　　　Yes or No

Ways I Care For My Friends:

_____

_____

_____

_____

Notes

FRIENDSHIP GOALS

DIG DEEPER

I have experienced hurt in this area.   Yes   or   No
(circle answer)

What do I need from my friendships?

How will I know I am healed?

Friendship Goals:

_____

_____

_____

_____

I forgive...

Notes

Notes

Notes

FINANCIAL GOALS

I WILL CONTROL THE MANAGEMENT OF MY MONEY

	Current	Goal
Monthly Income		
Savings		
Checking		
Monthly Expenses (total)		

Areas I Do Well With Money:

_____

_____

_____

Steps To Improve My Finances:

_____

_____

_____

Notes

FINANCIAL GOALS

DIG DEEPER

My biggest struggle with finances is:
(be honest. review your previous page to help)

Lessons finances have taught me:

_____

_____

_____

Notes

Notes

Notes

CAREER GOALS

I WILL CONFIDENTLY USE MY TALENTS AND RESOURCES MINDFULLY.

I WILL BE PRODUCTIVE AND EFFICIENT WITH MY TIME.

Goals:

-
-
-
-
-

Steps to Acheive My Goals:

-
-
-
-

My Successes Are:

-
-
-
-

Notes

CAREER GOALS

DIG DEEPER

The talents I will use to reach my goals are:

The workplace has taught me:

I know that I have reached my career goals when:
(identify at least 2 specific ways)

-
-

Notes

Notes

Notes

SELF-CARE

I WILL PUT MYSELF FIRST WHEN I AM FEELING STRESSED AND OVERWHELMED.

Do you practice self-care?   Yes   or   No
(circle answer)

What do you currently do to take care of yourself?

_____

_____

_____

_____

My current self-care practice has taught me:

-

-

Notes

SELF-CARE

Dig Deeper

You cannot pour from an empty cup. Fill yourself up so you can "Be the Best You".

SELF-CARE
TO DO LIST

Self-care is a key component to feeling renewed.

Its often an act that replaces self-neglect. It needs to be intentional. If you want to make sure that you are putting your mental, emotional, physical, and spiritual well-being first, use the Self-Care To Do List.

This list will be your guide. As you go about your every day life, it will serve as a reminder to do one of your self-care items on your list. Be sure to include both simple and challenging self-care tasks. For example, painting your nails is a fairly simple task, where scheduling a massage may require a bit more planning. Give yourself some grace, you do not have to complete this in a certain time frame. Schedule your "me time" if needed. Make yourself a priority.

Keep it simple and be kind to yourself.

Print or Copy the following Self-Care worksheets. Write down ways to practice self-care and check it off as completed.

SELF-CARE
SUGGESTED ACTIVITIES:

- Take a hot bath with Epsom salt and lavender scented candles
- Do a guided meditation video
- Connect with a good friend
- Take a 30 minute walk
- Use a diffuser with your favorite essential oils
- Have a warm cup of tea
- Fill a vase with fresh flowers
- Participate in an online book club
- Take a dance class (online or in-person)
- Try a meditation app such as Calm
- Donate your time to volunteer
- Create a self-care vision board
- Start a gratitude journal
- Make yourself a tasty treat
- Learn to cook a healthy meal
- Watch an online concert
- Declutter your bedroom
- Clear off your social media feed from negative energy
- Organize your finances
- Create something unique and crafty
- Take an art class
- Write or draw about your emotions in a journal
- Spend time in nature
- Take a personal-development class/course
- Make a healthy smoothie

To Do List:
BE KIND TO YOURSELF

TASK | S M T W TH F S

NOTES

To Do List:
BE KIND TO YOURSELF

TASK S M T W TH F S

NOTES

To Do List:
BE KIND TO YOURSELF

TASK   S   M   T   W   TH   F   S

_____

_____

_____

_____

_____

_____

_____

_____

_____

_____

_____

_____

NOTES

Notes

Monthly Reflections

THE FOLLOWING PAGES PROVIDED ARE FOR REFLECTION AT THE END OF THE MONTH. WRITE IN YOUR ANSWERS AND TAKE NOTES FOR ADDITIONAL THOUGHTS.

Monthly Reflections

I will give myself compassion and grace for
what I am able to accomplish

FAVORITE AFFIRMATION(S):

MY BEST ACCOMPLISHMENTS:

THIS MONTH I LEARNED...

Notes

Monthly Reflections

I will give myself compassion and grace for what I am able to accomplish

FAVORITE AFFIRMATION(S):

MY BEST ACCOMPLISHMENTS:

THIS MONTH I LEARNED...

Notes

Monthly Reflections

I will give myself compassion and grace for
what I am able to accomplish

FAVORITE AFFIRMATION(S):

MY BEST ACCOMPLISHMENTS:

THIS MONTH I LEARNED...

Notes

Monthly Reflections

I will give myself compassion and grace for what I am able to accomplish

FAVORITE AFFIRMATION(S):

MY BEST ACCOMPLISHMENTS:

THIS MONTH I LEARNED...

Notes

Monthly Reflections

I will give myself compassion and grace for
what I am able to accomplish

FAVORITE AFFIRMATION(S):

MY BEST ACCOMPLISHMENTS:

THIS MONTH I LEARNED...

Notes

Monthly Reflections

I will give myself compassion and grace for what I am able to accomplish

FAVORITE AFFIRMATION(S):

MY BEST ACCOMPLISHMENTS:

THIS MONTH I LEARNED...

Notes

Monthly Reflections

I will give myself compassion and grace for
what I am able to accomplish

FAVORITE AFFIRMATION(S):

MY BEST ACCOMPLISHMENTS:

THIS MONTH I LEARNED...

Notes

Monthly Reflections

I will give myself compassion and grace for
what I am able to accomplish

FAVORITE AFFIRMATION(S):

MY BEST ACCOMPLISHMENTS:

THIS MONTH I LEARNED...

Notes

Monthly Reflections

I will give myself compassion and grace for
what I am able to accomplish

FAVORITE AFFIRMATION(S):

MY BEST ACCOMPLISHMENTS:

THIS MONTH I LEARNED...

Notes

Monthly Reflections

I will give myself compassion and grace for what I am able to accomplish

FAVORITE AFFIRMATION(S):

MY BEST ACCOMPLISHMENTS:

THIS MONTH I LEARNED...

Notes

Monthly Reflections

I will give myself compassion and grace for
what I am able to accomplish

FAVORITE AFFIRMATION(S):

MY BEST ACCOMPLISHMENTS:

THIS MONTH I LEARNED...

Notes

Monthly Reflections

I will give myself compassion and grace for
what I am able to accomplish

FAVORITE AFFIRMATION(S):

MY BEST ACCOMPLISHMENTS:

THIS MONTH I LEARNED...

Notes

Notes

Notes

Notes

Notes

Notes

Notes

Notes

Notes

Notes

Notes

Notes

Notes

Notes

Notes

CONTINUE TO
Heal & Renew

By using this workbook as a tool, you have successfully began your healing journey. Continue your new and positive habits. Learn from any mistakes and experiences you encountered throughout your journey. Keep this workbook handy as a reference when you need to overcome a painful situation and rejuvenate yourself. *Heal and Renew* with purposeful and intentional practices.

The following pages are optional resources for you. Go to www.positivesteps10.com for additional resources and information.
Check out our podcast:

(c) 2020 All Rights Reserved

MY RENEW PLEDGE

HEALING, FOR ME, IS INTENTIONAL.

I will commit myself to the process of healing by doing the following:

By This Date:

Create my healing playlist

Create my healing watchlist

Purge negative energy and items from my space

Other _____

Other _____

_____
(Signature)

_____
(Date)

"I give you peace, the kind of peace only I can give. So don't be worried or afraid"
John 14:27

LIST OF
Coping Skills

Listen to relaxing music

Be alone for a while

Positive Self-talk

Listen to a motivational podcast or video

Be creative

Exercise

Draw or color

Cook something

Work on your craft

Write a pros and cons list

Volunteer your time

Aromatherapy

Call a friend

Say "No"

Try using Mindfulness techniques

Write in a journal

Slow down

Have a good cry

Deep breathing

Rest

Dance or sing

Body Scan

Organize your space

Say "Yes"

APPENDIX A

Here are some suggestions to include in your playlists, watchlist, and books to read.
Add titles that relate to your personal life.

RENEW music playlist:

"Cranes in the Sky" by Solange
"Stronger Than Pride" by Sade
"Breathe" by Byron Cage
"No Weapon" by Fred Hammond

RENEW watchlist:

Eat, Pray, Love (2010)
Love Jones (1997)
Soulfood (1997)
This is Us (2016)
Becoming (2020)

RENEW books:

The Big Book of Little Lies by Tina Lifford
The Color of Hope by Iresha Picot
Healing for Damaged Emotions by David Seamans
Healing the Soul of a Woman by Joyce Meyers

Podcast playlist:

PS10 Radio
H.E.R. Space
Woman Evolve
Declutter Empress

RESOURCES TO
Heal & Renew

These resources include mental health entities.

National Helpline: 1-800-662-HELP

National Suicide Prevention Lifeline: 1-800-273-8255

Crisis Text line: 741741

Therapist directories:
www.psychologytoday.com
www.blacktherapistsrock.com
www.therapyforblackgirls.com
www.goodtherapy.org
www.directoryfortherapists.com
members.adaa.org

Thank you

www.ingramcontent.com/pod-product-compliance
Lightning Source LLC
Chambersburg PA
CBHW081519160426
43193CB00015B/2736